KNOWABOUT

Pattern

© 1994 Watts Books

Watts Books
96 Leonard Street
London EC2A 4RH

Franklin Watts Australia
14 Mars Road
Lane Cove
NSW 2066

ISBN: 0 7496 1672 5

Dewey Decimal Classification 513

10 9 8 7 6 5 4 3 2 1

A CIP catalogue record for this book
is available from the British Library.

Editor: Ruth Thomson
Design: Chloë Cheesman

Additional photographs: Laura Ashley 12;
Axminster Carpets Ltd 13; Eye Ubiquitous
© Roger Chester 22; Robert Harding Picture
Library 17, © Walter Rawlings 8; ZEFA 24, 25.

Printed in Hong Kong

KNOWABOUT

Pattern

Text: Henry Pluckrose
Photography: Chris Fairclough

Watts Books
London • New York • Sydney

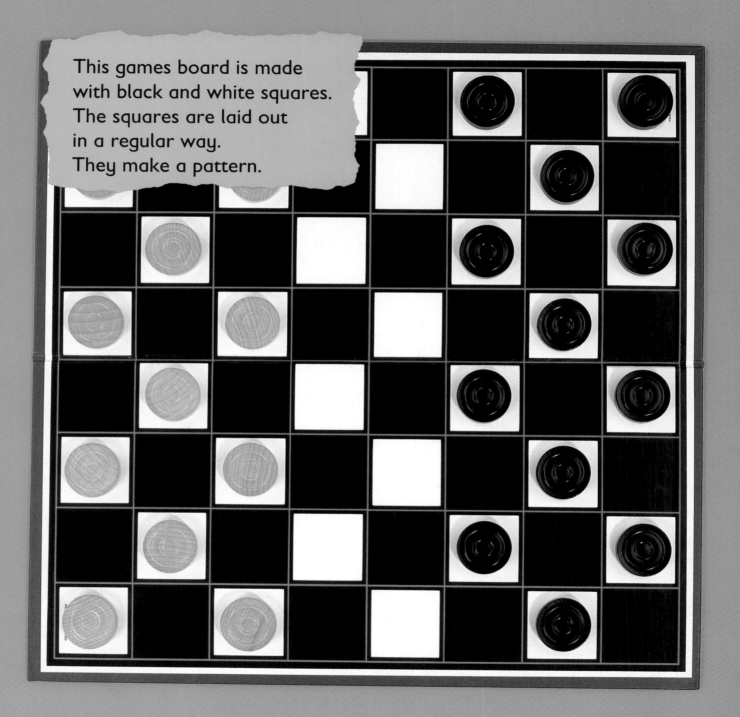

This games board is made
with black and white squares.
The squares are laid out
in a regular way.
They make a pattern.

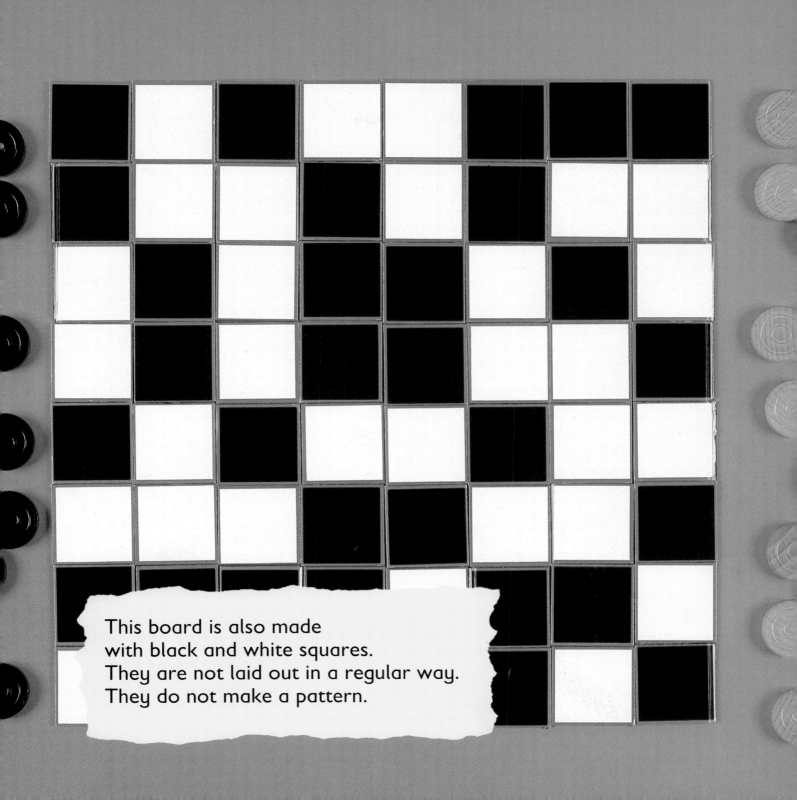

This board is also made
with black and white squares.
They are not laid out in a regular way.
They do not make a pattern.

Patterns are all around us.
You can find patterns in nature -
on the heads and petals of flowers . . .

on leaves . . .

on birds . . .

and butterflies.
Is the pattern on each wing
of the butterfly exactly the same?

There is a spiral pattern on this shell ...

and a pattern of stripes
on the coat of the zebra.

We decorate our homes
with patterned wallpaper and fabric.

We put patterned carpets on the floor.

We eat from patterned dishes ...

and plates.

Things we wear
are often patterned ...

and so are clothes
worn on special occasions.

Many patterns repeat themselves.
Can you see the repeat
in this pattern?

Some patterns repeat themselves
in a different way.
How does this pattern repeat itself?

There are patterns almost everywhere. What shapes repeat themselves in these cranes to make a pattern?

What pattern can you see in these cobbles?

Some shapes fit together tightly
to make a pattern . . .

and some leave little spaces.
The spaces make a pattern too!

These swimmers are making a pattern with their bodies.

The water makes a circular pattern when a drop hits its surface.

This is a close-up of a car tyre.
Why does it have this pattern?

There is also a pattern on the sole of this shoe. How does the pattern help prevent the runner from slipping?

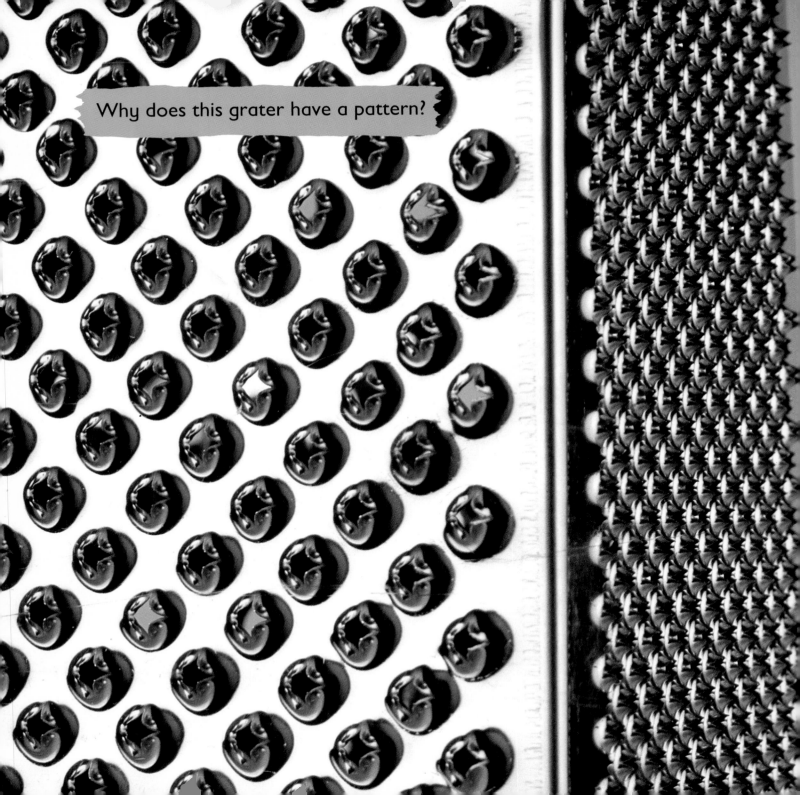

Why does this grater have a pattern?

The spiral pattern
on the rope
gives the climber
a good grip.

Look around you.

How many different patterns can you see?

About this book

This book is designed for use in the home, playgroup and infant school.

Mathematics is a part of the child's world. It is not just about interpreting numbers or in mastering the tricks of addition or multiplication. Mathematics is about *Ideas*. These ideas (or concepts) have been developed over the centuries to help explain particular qualities, such as size, weight, height, as well as relationships and comparisons. Yet all too often the important part which an understanding of mathematics will play in a child's development is forgotten or ignored.

Most adults can solve simple mathematical tasks by "doing them in their head." For example you can probably add up or subtract simple numbers without the need for counters, beads or fingers. Young children find such abstractions almost impossible to master. They need to see, talk, touch and experiment.

The photographs in this book and the text which supports them have been prepared with one major aim. They have been chosen to encourage talk around topics which are essentially mathematical. By talking with you, the young reader will be helped to explore some of the central concepts which underpin mathematics. It is upon an understanding of these concepts that a child's future mastery of mathematics will be built.

Henry Pluckrose